The Hastings Hours

Memoria de sancto dauid
confessor. Antiphona
st est qui ante
deum magnas
virtutes opa
tus est et omis

The
Hastings
Hours

Janet Backhouse

THE BRITISH LIBRARY

INTIMATE IN SCALE and richly decorated with miniatures from the life of Christ and of the saints, set off by delicate flower paintings and occasional light-hearted glimpses of contemporary courtly life, the Hastings Hours embodies most popular expectations of a luxury illuminated manuscript from the late Middle Ages. The book was made in the southern Netherlands during the last quarter of the fifteenth century by expert craftsmen of the famous school of illumination centred on the Flemish towns of Ghent and Bruges. The original patron is identified by his arms as William Lord Hastings, close friend and staunch supporter of King Edward IV of England, who was summarily executed in June 1483 at the orders of Richard III. The Hours must therefore have been written and illuminated about 1480. Almost completely unknown before it was bequeathed to the nation in 1968 by Mrs F.W.M. Perrins, this manuscript is now recognised as a key work in the early development of what was to prove one of the last great flowerings of an essentially medieval art form.

During the fifteenth century the southern Netherlands, an area roughly equivalent to modern Belgium, was a focal point for international trade and supported communities of merchants from both northern and southern Europe. It was also the home of the Burgundian ducal court, renowned for its patronage of the arts and for its luxurious and sophisticated life-style. These factors combined to encourage a lively trade in all kinds of luxury goods such as pictures, tapestries and illuminated books. The works of Flemish craftsmen were widely desired and made their way into most parts of Europe. Links with neighbouring England were particularly close, largely owing to the wool trade, and the political relationship was strengthened in 1468 when Edward IV's younger sister Margaret became the wife of the Burgundian Duke Charles, amid wedding celebrations of a magnificence that dazzled their contemporaries.

The Book of Hours was the popular manual of private devotion during the late Middle Ages. Its essential component is a series of eight short services in honour of the Virgin Mary, designed to be recited at different times of the day, hence the name. Each service consists of a combination of psalms, prayers, readings and hymns after the pattern of the daily Office set out in the Breviary for the use of the regular clergy, but in a simplified form that takes no account of the seasonal variations that are followed by professional devotions. Minor textual variations do however distinguish the preferred 'use' of different regions, making it possible to localise the books. In England the use of Sarum (Salisbury) was commonly followed, though there are some books of the use of

Overleaf

1
St Christopher
(f. 48b)

2
Memorial of
St Christopher
(f. 49)

Memoria de sco vristoro. ant

sancte vristo
ir martir
ils su vristi
qui pro eius
nomine per
na pertuli sti opem confer mi
sere atque mundo tristi. qui
celeste glorie regna manus
vristofori sancti speciem qui ca
que tuetur illo nempe die nul
lo sanguine gravetur. confer
solamen et mentis tolle gra
uamen. Judicis examen fac
mite sit omnibus. ꝟ Ora
pro nobis beate martir vristo

York, usually associated with patrons from the north of the country. The Hastings Hours is of Sarum use and it would therefore be clear that it was intended for an English owner even if evidence of the patron's identity were lacking. The basic text of the Hours is normally accompanied by a number of other ingredients. The first of these is frequently a calendar, indicating saints' days throughout the year. The inclusion of unusual names often gives additional clues to the manuscript's original destination. Typically there may also be extracts from the four gospels, further sequences of Hours to honour the Passion, the Cross or the Holy Spirit, the Penitential Psalms with a litany of saints, the Office of the Dead, and prayers and memorials addressed to individual saints. In a grand book such as the Hastings Hours, each different section is likely to be introduced by an appropriate illustration. In Flemish manuscripts these were usually painted on separate leaves of vellum inserted into the volume when it was bound up and thus easily removed or lost later in its history.

The Hastings Hours accords closely to this pattern. It opens with a calendar (ff.1–12b) in which a large number of English saints is included, together with many names from the Netherlands and northern France. Many such calendars are lavishly decorated with tiny miniatures of the occupations of the months and the signs of the zodiac but this one, disap-

3
Border detail
from the
Memorial of
St George
(f. 47)

teorgie.

vpi glo
t laue
tutor an
flere gē
amiose
ac discor:
on cordie

pointingly, is unadorned. The book's main text opens with gospel extracts (ff.13–17b) which must originally have been introduced by a miniature of St John the Evangelist, though this is now missing. These are followed by a very long series of individual devotions (ff.19–72), opening with a prayer to Christ and a memorial of the Holy Trinity and including memorials for twenty-two separate saints, each originally accompanied by an illustration. Six of these have been lost. Next comes the Hours of the Virgin (ff.74–149b), punctuated by eight miniatures from the story of the birth and infancy of Christ, then the Penitential Psalms, Gradual Psalms and litany (ff.151–183b), the Office of the Dead (ff.185–229b), the Commendation of Souls (ff.231–249), the Psalms of the Passion (ff.251–264b), the Fifteen "Oes" attributed to St Bridget of Sweden (ff.266–275b) and the Psalter of St Jerome (ff.276–297b), each introduced by a suitable miniature.

The text of the Hastings Hours was written out, sixteen lines to the page, by an accomplished scribe whose hand has been recognised in several other outstanding manuscripts of the period. His participation provides a link between several particularly talented illuminators. The chosen script is typical of professionally produced manuscripts of its time and place. Being semi-cursive, it could doubtless have been executed at considerable speed. Minor divisions in the text are

Overleaf

4
St Anthony of Egypt
(f. 50b)

5
St Erasmus
(f. 53b)

6
Memorial of St Erasmus: Maying
(f. 54)

11

Memoria de sancto Serasino.

S u sape me scē
serasine in tu
am fidem et
gratiam et con
serua me per
hos octo dies ab omni malo
et presta michi peragere ai
uera fide et omni prosperita
te et gratia finem bonum vi
te mee vt non proficiat mine
ulla inimicorum voluntatis
tibi ad laudem et honorem in
consolationem et gratiam ti
bi sancte serasine commendo
corpus meum et animam meam

marked by small decorative initials and each major section begins with a large capital, six lines high, in red, gold, blue and white against a ground of burnished gold. The original binding has long since disappeared but this is the kind of personal book that might well have been covered in richly coloured velvet with a large protective chemise and clasps and ornaments of precious metal. Such bindings may frequently be seen on books held by figures of the saints in contemporary Flemish panel paintings. Within the manuscript itself one example appears in the miniature of St Sitha (12) and a second may be seen lying in front of the Virgin in the miniature of the Annunciation (16).

In its original state the Hastings Hours contained a total of thirty-nine large miniatures. Twenty-five are reproduced here on a scale very close to that of the original. All but four of these miniatures were painted, according to local custom, on separate leaves left blank on the unillustrated side. Each miniature is enclosed in a decorative border, usually of floral ornament, and the text which it was designed to face has complementary decoration. Seven miniatures, all relating to devotions at the beginning of the manuscript, are now lost but decorated text pages mark the points at which they once appeared. The four miniatures which do not fit in to this regular pattern occupy a separate group of four single leaves in the early part of the volume (ff.38–41b). They are not accompanied by decorated text pages. Instead each has the opening words of the relevant text immediately below it. These four miniatures represent the saints Paul, Leonard, David of Wales (frontispiece) and Jerome. Their position in the manuscript, ahead of all the other individual saints, and the departure of these pages from the otherwise very regular design pattern of the book, must suggest that they had some special significance for the original patron and that their inclusion was the result of a direct instruction. The majority of the other chosen saints were universally venerated and are commonly to be found in books such as this. The only distinctly English saint is Thomas Becket (7), though the high position given to St George, third in line after John the Baptist in the basic sequence, may reflect his status as England's traditional patron. Unfortunately his is one of the miniatures that has been lost.

All the miniatures are exquisitely painted. In many of them figures in contemporary dress play the subsidiary roles in biblical episodes or in crucial moments from the lives of the saints, which would have given the subjects an immediacy no longer apparent to the modern eye. This is particularly well demonstrated in the martyrdom of St Erasmus (5), in the scene of St Elizabeth giving alms to the poor (11), in the Adoration of the Magi (22) and in the Massacre of the Innocents

(26). Contemporary northern architecture and landscape is used to similar effect as a background to the Visitation (18), to King David kneeling in penitence (27), to Christ washing the feet of his disciples (31) and to St Jerome with his lion and his donkey (32). Many of the compositions found in the Hastings Hours were re-used in later books from the Ghent-Bruges workshops and became familiar over a long period. The most striking of the compositions making its debut here is the dramatic evocation accompanying the Commendation of Souls (30), in which naked figures of the dead are transported into heaven by a host of angels. The Almighty, arms outstretched, leans down towards them. Below extends a segment of the firmament, its brilliant blue surface adorned with sun and stars.

7
St Thomas
Becket
(f. 55b)

During the later Middle Ages the production of fine illuminated manuscripts was a very professional business, involving teams of craftsmen, each specialising in some particular aspect of the work. It is often possible to distinguish different hands in different parts of the decoration, with a master hand responsible for the main miniatures which were the crowning glory of the finished commission. In the Hastings Hours, however, the border decoration is so sensitively designed to complement the illustrations, particularly in the choice of colouring for the marginal decoration on the text

pages, that it seems likely that a single hand was responsible for the entire decorative scheme of the manuscript. This is one of the earliest manuscripts in which borders filled entirely with illusionistic flower paintings are to be found. Every one of these deserves to be reproduced and it is very hard to choose which merits special attention. The wonderful display of irises (front cover) which was designed to accompany the miniature of the Flight into Egypt (25) is certainly one of the most striking in the volume. The mixed blooms surrounding the memorial to St Christopher (2) are handled with particular delicacy. The care taken over the choice of colouring is best recognised in the borders to the miniatures of St Margaret (10), where the salmon shade of the pinks reflects the tone of the saint's mantle, and St Katherine (15), where pinks and wild roses on a blue ground echo the predominant colours of the composition. The inclusion of stylised acanthus leaves in the latter border and on a number of the other flower pages, looks back to the style of marginal decoration current in the same neighbourhood during previous decades. The independent flower paintings seem to have been a development of the last two or three years of the 1470s.

On four pages the marginal decoration takes an entirely different form. These are so arranged that the panel of plain vellum containing the text appears to be superimposed upon a

full page picture of a scene from contemporary life. The first of these (back cover), which faces a miniature of the Adoration of the Magi and introduces an unusual memorial for the Three Kings, depicts a group of fashionably dressed citizens striving to catch or gather up a cascade of gold coins being rained down upon them by two figures at the top of the page. This composition was subsequently many times re-used, in some instances with flower heads in place of the coins. Some ten leaves further into the manuscript, accompanying the memorial for St Erasmus (5), another page is adorned with a boating scene (6). The branch in the prow of the little vessel suggests that its occupants have been out on May Morning to collect the traditional greenery to decorate their houses, a scene very often found in Flemish calendars to represent the month of May. The young couple in the forepart of the boat are making music, the older figure in the stern is drinking from a large bottle. The miniaturist has given full rein to his talent in depicting rippling water and reflections from the tall buildings. Careful scrutiny reveals not only crowds of tiny people in other more distant boats but also minute figures in almost all the windows. A third pictorial border (13) appears opposite the miniature of St Sitha (Zita of Lucca; 12). A fool and two ladies wearing the fashionable steeple head-dresses of the day, one seemingly reassuring the other, attend a joust between

two knights, perhaps their personal champions. The horse trappings of one are besprinkled with golden teardrops. The other carries the motto BASIR ('kiss'). The fourth contemporary scene, once again featuring boats and water, has a specifically English flavour (24). Opposite a miniature of the Presentation of Christ in the Temple, introducing the Office for None (23), eight strangely hooded figures are rowing a barge, in the bows of which two trumpeters sound instruments bearing banners of the royal arms of England. An impossibly large pennant at the vessel's prow, which in real life would inevitably capsize it, has the opening word of the motto of the Order of the Garter, 'HONI [soit qui mal y pense]', inscribed in letters of gold on a ground of red and blue. Similar pennants appear in the margins of manuscripts made in the Low Countries for Edward IV at this time.

10
St Magaret
(f. 62b)

The illuminator responsible for this beautiful, colourful and accomplished work remains anonymous, though his very recognisable style is to be found in a considerable number of other manuscripts made in the Burgundian Netherlands during the last quarter of the fifteenth century. He was one of a small group of book painters of outstanding brilliance and originality, almost all equally anonymous, who specialised in particular in the production of luxury Books of Hours and were patronised by the inner circle of the ducal court. The

member of this group who has attracted the most extensive study is known as the Master of Mary of Burgundy because of his association with manuscripts made for the young ruling Duchess Mary, stepdaughter of Edward IV's sister Margaret, who succeeded her father Charles when he was killed at the Battle of Nancy in January 1477. Others were the Master of the Dresden Prayerbook, who was particularly skilled in painting calendar miniatures and whose career reached its zenith some twenty years later in his contribution to the Breviary of Queen Isabella of Castile (BL, Additional MS 18851), and Simon Marmion, native of Valenciennes, whose talent was celebrated by name alongside Van Eyck and Van der Goes by the French poet Jean Lemaire in 1503. All these illuminators are associated with the new illusionistic style of floral border painting seen in the Hastings Hours. They appear side by side in varying combinations in the same manuscripts and some of them are linked together through the work of the scribe responsible for the Hastings Hours. Their patrons included not only Duchess Mary herself but also her husband Maximilian of Austria, afterwards successively King of the Romans and Holy Roman Emperor, whom she married in the summer of 1477, and her cousins and close associates Engelbert of Nassau and Philip of Cleves. Mary died as the result of a hunting accident in 1482, Hastings was

11
St Elizabeth
(f. 64b)

Overleaf

12
*St Sitha or
Zita of Lucca
f. 66b)*

13
*Memorial of
St Sitha:
Jousting
(f. 67)*

Memoria de sancta sitha. an

A ue sancta
famula
sitha xpū
vpī. Que
cum tota
anima:

deo placuisti. Egenos et fle
biles de albo fouisti. Cecos
mutos debiles et claudos i
uisti. Semper elemosinam
dare quesiuisti. Deum et
ecclesiam virgo dilexisti
fraudem et nequiciam tu
nimis odisti. Para nobis
gloriam quam tu meru

executed in 1483 and Philip of Cleves apparently varied his personal identification marks in or about 1485, so several of the manuscripts can be very closely dated.

Our own artist has been christened the Master of the Older Prayerbook of Maximilian I, in honour of a manuscript now in the Austrian National Library in Vienna (Cod. 1907) which was apparently made for Duchess Mary's widower at about the time of his election as King of the Romans in 1486. It is not impossible that he was in fact Alexander Bening, father of the celebrated Simon who was to become the most famous and successful illuminator of the first half of the sixteenth century. Alexander Bening's career is quite well documented but he cannot so far be linked to any recognisable works. However, a number of compositions used by our artist were certainly re-used by Simon Bening and passed on to his contemporaries.

The identities of the major patrons of this small group of illuminators put the original owner of the Hastings Hours among a very elevated class. The significance of the manuscript as a witness to the early development of the late fifteenth century Ghent-Bruges style depends upon its apparently early dating and this dating itself depends upon the perceived association of the manuscript with William Lord Hastings, whose execution in June 1483 provides a terminal date for

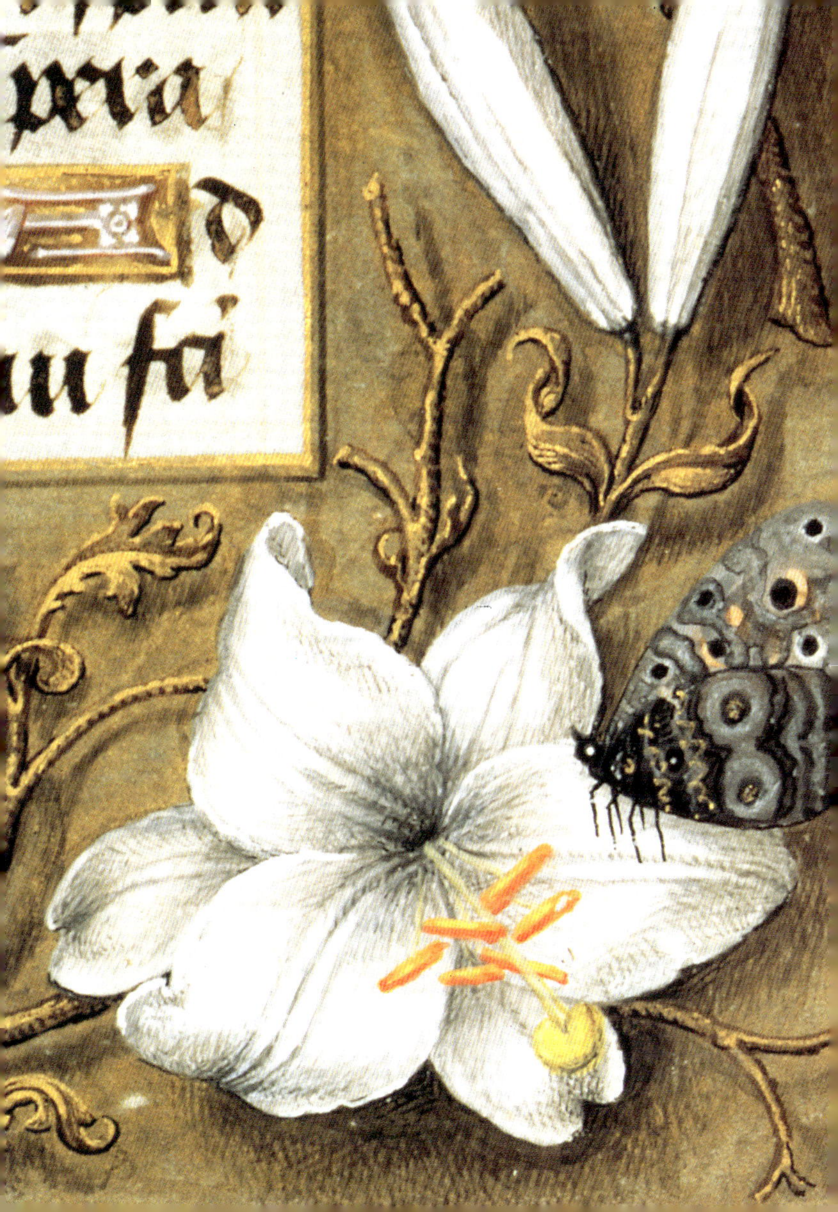
pria
d
u fi

its production. Nothing in the style or contents of the book is inconsistent with such a date, but by birth Hastings could certainly not have aspired to membership of such a company. He was the son of Sir Leonard Hastings of Kirby Muxloe in Leicestershire and Burton Hastings in Warwickshire, an adherent of the party of Richard Duke of York and his family, who died in 1455. Hastings himself was born about 1430 and was associated from an early age with York and his sons, afterwards Edward IV and Richard III respectively. In December 1460 the Duke, having formally claimed the English crown, was killed at Wakefield along with his second son, Edmund Earl of Rutland, and many of his leading supporters. Hastings, now aged about thirty, was with York's eighteen-year-old heir Edward at the crucial Battle of Towton on 29 March 1461, where decisive victory assured him of Henry VI's crown. He was the first of Edward's companions to be dubbed knight on the battlefield by the new king, whose close friend and companion he was to remain throughout the reign, and his rise to power thereafter was meteoric. In the summer he was raised to the peerage and the following March he was named a Knight of the Order of the Garter, Europe's premier order of chivalry. Large estates, including Ashby-de-la-Zouche in Leicestershire, were granted to him, many of them from the lands forfeited by the Lancastrian supporters of

15
St Katherine
(f. 68b)

Overleaf

16
The Annunciation
(f. 73b)

17
Matins of the Hours of the Virgin
(f. 74)

Incipiunt hore beatissime
marie virginis secundum
usum sarum. Ad matutinas

D omine la
bia mea a
pies. Et
os meum
annuncia
bit lau

dem tuam

D eus in adiutorium
meum intende. Dne
ad adiuuandum me festina
Gloria patri et filio et spi
ritu sancto. Sicut erat in
principio et nunc et semper

Henry VI, and many of the royal strongholds in the Midlands and North Wales were placed in his hands. He became, among other things, Chamberlain of the Royal Household, Master and Worker of the King's Mints, Receiver-General of the Duchy of Cornwall and Chamberlain of North Wales, each appointment assuring him of considerable material profits.

Early in the summer of 1461 he also made a brilliant marriage to Katherine Neville, widow of William Bonville, Lord Harington. She was a daughter of Richard Neville, Earl of Salisbury, and sister of Richard Neville, Earl of Warwick (afterwards to be known as 'the Kingmaker'), both of whom had been among York's most prominent allies. Her two grandmothers, Joan Beaufort, Countess of Westmorland and Eleanor Holland, Countess of Salisbury, were both of royal blood and she herself was Edward IV's first cousin on his mother's side. Through the marriages of her numerous siblings she was related to most of the leading families in the kingdom. In addition to her own dowry, she brought to the marriage the wardship of her infant daughter, Cecily Bonville, sole heir to the Baronies of both Harington and Bonville and to enormous estates in the west of England. Katherine had suffered multiple bereavements in the months before Towton, losing her husband, her father-in-law, her own father and one brother as a result of Wakefield. Her first husband's grandfather was beheaded by order of Queen Margaret of Anjou on the day after the Battle of St Albans in February 1461. Her marriage to Hastings lasted more than twenty years and she was to survive him by a further two decades, dying in old age in 1503.

During the first part of Edward IV's reign, Hastings undertook numerous diplomatic missions, several of which took him to the Burgundian Netherlands. In particular he was involved in the negotiations which preceded Margaret of York's marriage to Duke Charles in 1468. Two years later he was one of the small group that accompanied Edward into exile in the Low Countries during Henry VI's brief restoration to the throne in 1470–1. The refugees were entertained by Louis of Gruthuyse, governor of Holland and a former ambassador to England, first at his residence in the Hague and later at his house in Bruges. Gruthuyse was a celebrated bibliophile and his love of fine manuscripts and patronage of some of the best illuminators of the day can hardly have gone unnoticed by his guests. His hospitality was afterwards repaid by Edward, who invited him to Windsor in the autumn of 1472 and created him Earl of Winchester. On that occasion Hastings, in his capacity as Chamberlain of the Royal Household, and his brother-in-law, Sir John Donne, were entrusted with the initial welcome. During the second half of the reign

Overleaf

18
The Visitation
(f. 85b)

19
Lauds of the Hours of the Virgin
(f. 86)

Ad laudes.
Deus in ad
iutorium
meum inté
de. Domine
ad adiuuā
dum me festina ⚜ Gloria
patri et filio. et spū sancto
ꝯ rait erat in principio
et nunc et semper et in secula
seculorum Amen. Antiphō
O admirabile pūe
Domine regnauit
decorem induit est induit
est dominus fortitudinem
et precinxit se ⚜ Et tenīn

Hastings maintained his place close to the king and his power and influence continued to grow. In 1471 the important post of Lieutenant of Calais was added to his many official functions, giving him permanent continental interests and access. He remained unswervingly loyal to his royal friend and master and that loyalty seems at once to have been transferred to Edward's heir, the ill-fated Edward V, when the king died at the early age of forty in April 1483. From 1473 Hastings had indeed been among those designated tutors and councillors to the young prince. It was probably this loyalty which proved his eventual downfall, for within a matter of weeks his standpoint was seen to be too great a stumbling block in the path mapped out by Edward's brother, Richard Duke of Gloucester, Lord Protector of England. On 13 June 1483 his execution was summarily ordered and by the end of that month the Lord Protector was King Richard III. Hastings was buried, as he had wished, in St George's Chapel at Windsor, next to his royal friend. His widow, by royal clemency, was not in the long term deprived of his estates.

The principal evidence connecting William Lord Hastings with the Hastings Hours is heraldic. The book does however fit in very well with his known activities as a patron of the arts and with the general framework of his career. A date of around 1480 or slightly before is consistent with the

stylistic evidence offered by the manuscript. This coincides with major building projects at Ashby-de-la-Zouche, where Hastings constructed a very ambitious tower house during the later 1470s and made substantial additions to the other accommodation, and at Kirby Muxloe, where work on the new and fashionably brick-built moated castle, never completed, was initiated late in 1480. The new buildings and their contents, as mirrored in the provisions of Lady Hastings's will, drawn up in November 1503, would clearly have been appropriate to their owner's increasingly exalted status. The appearance of a sketch for his arms in a volume of Froissart's *Chronicle* now among the Royal manuscripts (BL, Royal MS 18 E. i) may indicate that he shared Edward's interest in the purchase of de luxe library books from the Flemish workshops. Edward's activities in this direction are well known and seem to have been concentrated in the years 1479–80, when he was collecting other accessories such as tapestries in parallel with his own building activities at Windsor, where St George's chapel was begun in 1475, and at Eltham. Close contacts with the Burgundian ducal court were renewed at this time, during the period of Duchess Mary's accession and marriage, and the Dowager Duchess Margaret paid a formal visit to London in 1480. Among the ambassadors to Flanders in 1477 was Hastings's brother-in-law, Sir John Donne, who

21
The Annunciation to the Shepherds (f. 113b)

ordered a magnificent altarpiece (now in the National Gallery) from Hans Memling, Bruges's leading painter, and was also the owner of a number of fine illuminated manuscripts. It should not be forgotten that Caxton's *Mirror of the World*, completed in March 1481 and thus among the first books to be printed in England, is also associated with Hastings, translated from the French and published at the request of Hugh Bryce, Alderman of London and one of Hastings's long-term associates as Keeper of the Mint, for presentation to him.

The Hastings arms, *argent a maunch sable* (that is, a black stylised hanging sleeve on a silver ground), appear on four separate pages in the Hastings Hours and in three instances (half title page, 17 and 28) they are enclosed within the Garter. On the fourth occasion, in the funeral miniature (29), they are to be found as tiny details on the catafalque and on the hanging around the top of the chapel, where they are also painted on a banner. In each place it is quite clear that they have been added on top of decoration which had already been completed and this has led some scholars to suggest that they may as well refer to a later member of the family as to William himself. The inclusion of the Garter reduces the possible candidates to four. The first is William himself, installed in 1462 as we have already noted. The next member of the family to be so

Overleaf

22
The Adoration of the Magi
(f. 119b)

23
The Presentation of Christ in the Temple
(f. 125b)

24
None of the Hours of the Virgin: the royal barge
(f. 126)

Ad nonam

Deus in ad
iutorium
meum in
tende. Do
mine ad
adiuuandum me festina.

Gloria patri et filio. Im

Tem arator spe mentes
tuorum uisita imple
superna gratia que tu crasti
pectora Memento salutis
auctor quod nostri quondam
corporis ex illibata uirgine
nascendo formam sumpse
ris Maria mater gratie

honoured was his great-grandson, Francis Hastings, Earl of Huntingdon, in 1549. Francis's younger brother Edward received the Garter in 1555 and his son and successor, Henry Hastings, in 1570. There is however no necessity to propose that the arms are a sixteenth century addition. Many of the finest illuminated manuscripts produced to order in Flanders during the latter years of the fifteenth century contain no direct evidence of ownership at all. Hastings was the kind of person who might well have decided to have the arms added once the manuscript was in his possession. He does seem to have had a taste for using his arms decoratively on his buildings and other property. The maunch is outlined in the brickwork flanking the gatehouse at Kirby Muxloe and the will of Lady Hastings makes several references to soft furnishings bearing 'my Lordes Armes'. Particularly relevant in the present context is the very grand armorial decoration which occupies a niche high up on the northern face of the tower house at Ashby-de-la-Zouche, above the only surviving door. Although this is severely weathered, it is clear that the arms, below the crest and between the supporters, are surrounded by the ribbon of the Garter. The Garter also surrounds Hastings's arms on his Chantry at Windsor. Instances of personal arms surrounded by the Garter are not particularly common in manuscripts before the last years of the fifteenth century but the device was frequently used in stained glass at a much earlier period, so the examples in the Hastings Hours are entirely appropriate to William's ownership.

Several details of the contents of the manuscript, while none can be considered to offer conclusive evidence of ownership, do apparently tie in with William Hastings's known interests and connections. Three of the four saints included in the small inserted group at the beginning of the book may have had a special significance for him. St Paul, found here most unusually without St Peter, is the patron of the city of London's own cathedral church. Hastings had many links with the city, particularly through his responsibility for the Mint, and leased a house at St Paul's Wharf, the Thameside quay for the cathedral, from the Augustinian canons of St Bartholomew in Smithfield. Leonard, patron of prisoners, was his own father's name saint, and also the patron of the hospital in Leicester which Hastings granted to the collegiate church of our Lady there. David of Wales (frontispiece) reflects both his official connections with north Wales as Edward IV's representative and probably also his allegiance to Edward's young son and heir, created Prince of Wales in infancy. The miniature in this manuscript is apparently unique. Close scrutiny reveals that the standing figure of the saint was originally intended to be garbed as a bishop, which would have been suited to his life

story and to his status as patron of the principality, but was then transformed into a prince to accord with the legend of his royal birth. It is not clear why Hastings should have ordered the inclusion of the unusual memorial for the Three Kings, which follows immediately after the special group of saints, though their shrine at Cologne was a well known centre of pilgrimage. However, the marginal subject of the shower of gold, usually described as 'largesse' and reflecting a textual reference to the gift traditionally associated with the first of the Magi, can also be taken as a reference to Hastings who, as Master of the Mint, had been responsible for the introduction of the golden rose noble into the coinage.

25
*The Flight
into Egypt
(f. 131b)*

A strong connection with the English court is implicit at several places in the manuscript and has indeed in the past been interpreted as indicating an original royal owner, possibly the young Prince of Wales. Certainly the miniature of St David in the garb of a prince (frontispiece) would have been appropriate to him. The marginal scene of the barge (24), with its royal arms and Garter pennant, could also be significant. Perhaps most interesting of all is the fact that in the funeral miniature (29) the arms of Hastings can be seen, even in reproduction, to be painted over the royal arms of England. To modern eyes it may seem extremely insensitive, not to say potentially unlucky, to apply the arms and badges of a beloved

royal master or of one's own family to the trappings of a funeral scene. In the fifteenth century, however, a grand funeral followed by multiple masses for the repose of the soul of the deceased represented both a tribute to the exalted worldly status of the dead man and a ceremonial rite of passage, marking his final achievement of translation into the presence of God. The greater part of Hastings's own will, drawn up in 1481, is devoted to elaborate arrangements for prayers and masses to be said to ensure his welfare in the life hereafter. It includes specific instructions for the provision of his tomb at a place within St George's Chapel at Windsor assigned to him by Edward IV, near the spot where the king himself planned to be buried. The monuments of both men are in fact still to be seen there. The funeral miniature in the Hastings Hours is one of the compositions which was to be many times re-used by subsequent artists of the Ghent-Bruges school and in more than one instance spaces for arms were left blank, to be filled in at the patron's discretion. In one manuscript at least, the magnificent Hours commissioned by James IV of Scotland to mark his marriage to Margaret Tudor, daughter of Henry VII, in 1503 (Austrian National Library, Vienna, Cod. 1897), the arms of the book's owner have been placed in these spaces. There is no reason to interpret any of the royal symptoms in the Hastings Hours as anything more than a re-

26
*The Massacre
of the
Innocents
(f. 139b)*

Overleaf

27
*King David
before the
Almighty
(f. 150b)*

28
*The
Penitential
Psalms
(f. 151)*

Incipiunt septem psalmi p̄

Domine ne
in furore
tuo argu-
as me ne-
qȝ in ira
tua corripi-
as me Miserere mei domine
quoniam infirmus sum sa-
na me domine quoniam con-
turbata sunt omnia ossa
mea Et anima mea tur-
bata est valde sed tu domine
usquequo Convertere domine
et eripe animam meam sal-
uum me fac propter misericordiam

flection of its owner's allegiance to the royal house with which he was so closely associated.

The will of William Lord Hastings is not concerned with personal possessions and no books are mentioned in it. Two decades later Lady Hastings's will includes references to two 'primers' or Books of Hours among the chattels destined for particular members of her family. One, which was in the keeping of her sister Alice Lady Fitzhugh, was to be given to her daughter, Anne Hastings, and her husband, George, Earl of Shrewsbury. The other, which she had from Queen Elizabeth (though whether this means Elizabeth Wydeville, Edward IV's queen, or her daughter Elizabeth of York, the wife of Henry VII, is not specified), was destined for her eldest son, Edward Hastings, and his wife, the west-country heiress Mary Hungerford.

A second Book of Hours containing the Hastings arms does in fact exist and is now in the Museo Lazaro Galdiano in Madrid. It is furthermore almost exactly contemporary with the British Library manuscript. Although its miniatures are not the work of the Maximilian Master, they have been attributed to the Master of Mary of Burgundy. The text is written out by the same scribe and the content of the book, particularly the choice of saints favoured with special devotions (though the special group of Paul, Leonard, David and

Jerome is lacking), is remarkably similar. The arms of Hastings are placed at the beginning of the volume in the form of a full page composition, which appears to be a part of the original design of the book.

Strenuous attempts have inevitably been made to equate these two manuscripts with the two Books of Hours in Katherine Hastings's will. The history of the London manuscript is unfortunately entirely obscure from the time of its creation in the late fifteenth century until its reappearance in 1910. It was purchased by C.W. Dyson Perrins, a famous collector of illuminated books, from the London bookseller Bernard Quaritch for the then very large sum of £2,200. There is no record of the source from which Quaritch acquired it, though there is some reason to suspect that it may have come from a descendant of the Hastings family. It was included in a published catalogue of the Perrins collection in 1920 but failed to attract the sustained attention of scholars. When Dyson Perrins died in 1958 his collection was dispersed, largely through a series of record-breaking auction sales, but his widow chose to keep the Hastings Hours for herself. Its quality and freshness generated much surprise and delight when it was handed over to the British Museum's Department of Manuscripts on 8 February 1969, only a few weeks after her death, a great tribute to her taste and

perception. It is now numbered Additional MS 54782

The Hours in the Lazaro Galdiano collection offers rather more in the way of evidence, for it includes a number of additions made during the sixteenth and seventeenth centuries. The latest of these, dated 1659, records that the manuscript was given to the English Dominican community at Bornhem in Flanders by its founder, Philip Howard, brother of the 10th Duke of Norfolk, who was later to be created a cardinal by Pope Clement X. The earliest is an added group of leaves bearing a devotion to the Holy Trinity, introduced by a miniature in a style current in England at the very beginning of the sixteenth century. Associated border decoration incorporates the arms of the Earls of Arundel, Fitzalan quartering Maltravers. On the blank recto of the miniature of the Visitation in the body of the book (f.84) an inscription reads: 'When yow your prayers doo rehers Remembre Henry Mawtrevers'. This is apparently in the hand of Henry Fitzalan, a godson of Henry VIII, who bore the courtesy title of Lord Maltravers until he succeeded his father as Earl of Arundel in 1544. On the recto of the miniature of the Trinity attached to the added devotion (f.286), in the unmistakeable hand of Henry VIII's elder daughter, afterwards Mary I, a second inscription begs the prayers of a lady addressed as 'Myne owne good kate' on behalf of the princess 'whyche ame your lovyng mystres and ever

wyll be'. These additions have been interpreted as reflecting successive ownership of the manuscript, which would thus have passed from Henry Fitzalan to the princess and from her to a recipient who could perhaps be Katherine de la Pole, granddaughter of her beloved governess, the Countess of Salisbury. In 1532 Katherine was married to Francis Hastings, afterwards Earl of Huntingdon, to whom after 1549 the arms encircled by the Garter would have been appropriate.

It is however much more likely that both inscriptions were addressed to Henry Fitzalan's wife, Katherine Grey, whom he married about 1530. She was the granddaughter of William Hastings's stepdaughter, Cecily Bonville, married in 1474 to Thomas Grey, Marquess of Dorset, son of Edward IV's queen by her first marriage. Katherine, who died in 1542, seems to have been among Mary Tudor's ladies at a very early age, before the princess was stripped of her rank and status at the time of her half-sister Elizabeth's birth in 1533. Her elder daughter, named Mary in honour of the princess, married Thomas Howard, 4th Duke of Norfolk and was thus the great-great-grandmother of Cardinal Philip Howard. It was quite common in the late fifteenth and early sixteenth centuries for personal devotional books to be used as an early form of 'album amicorum' in this way. A particularly fine example is another Book of Hours (now BL Additional MS 17012),

the property of an unidentified lady of the Tudor court who collected inscriptions by numerous members of the royal family. The additions made to the Madrid Hastings Hours seem to offer a perfectly logical line of descent for the manuscript.

On available concrete evidence neither of the Hastings manuscripts can therefore be associated convincingly with either of the Books of Hours detailed in Lady Hastings's will. It is anyway unlikely that these were the only two examples of something as fashionable and as commonplace as a Book of Hours ever owned by Hastings and his extremely well-connected wife over a period of some forty years. In the years around 1480, when these manuscripts were commissioned, Hastings was at the zenith of his career, well established in the royal circle and financially prosperous. Between 1478 and the day on which he drafted his own will in 1481 his elder son and his daughter had both contracted extremely eligible alliances, the one with the heiress of the houses of Hungerford and Botreaux, the other with the young Earl of Shrewsbury, further strengthening his potential influence. Like the king himself, he was much engaged in demonstrating his position through his building works and other forms of artistic patronage. The commissioning of personal prayerbooks from the foremost suppliers of such commodities to the ducal court of Burgundy fits quite naturally into this general picture. A

31
Christ washing the feet of the Disciples
(f. 265b)

more delightful and desirable later medieval prayerbook than the London Hastings Hours would be hard to imagine. Hastings's sudden and brutal death has been immortalised by Shakespeare in *Richard III*. His life in the rich and elegant surroundings of the contemporary courts of England and Burgundy is commemorated in the pages of this enchanting manuscript.

32
St Jerome
(f. 278b)

Further Reading

D. H. Turner, The Hastings Hours, *Thames and Hudson, London, 1983.*

O. Pächt, The Master of Mary of Burgundy, *Faber and Faber, London, 1948.*

G. I. Lieftinck, Boekverluchters uit de Omgeving van Maria van Bourgondie c. 1475 – c. 1485, *Koninklijke Vlaamse Academie, Brussels, 1969.*

J. J. G. Alexander, The Master of Mary of Burgundy: a Book of Hours for Englebert of Nassau, *Phaidon Press, London, 1970.*

E. Inglis, The Hours of Mary of Burgundy, *Harvey Miller, London, 1995.*

T. Kren ed., Margaret of York, Simon Marmion, and 'Visions of Tondal', *J. Paul Getty Museum, Malibu, 1992.*

W. Prevenier and W. Blockmans, The Burgundian Netherlands, *Cambridge University Press, 1986.*

C. Ross, The Wars of the Roses, *Thames and Hudson, London, 1976 (pb 1986).*

Each of these books offers further bibliography.

Captions

Front cover: border detail of f. 132

Back cover: border detail of f. 43

Halftitle page: detail of the Hastings arms (f. 13)

Frontispiece: St David of Wales (f. 40)

Front endpaper: detail of f. 65

Back endpaper: detail of f. 107

©1996 The British Library Board

First published 1996 by

The British Library

Great Russell Street

London WC1B 3DG

British Library Cataloguing in Publication Data

A catalogue record for this title is available from The British Library

ISBN 0-7123-0439-8

Designed and typeset by Roger Davies

Colour origination by York House Graphics

Printed in Italy by Artegrafica, Verona

adiuuandum m

 coria patri

fpiritu fancto